PRINCEWILL LAGANG

Beyond the Boardroom: Insights into Michael Dell's Leadership and Innovation

First published by PRINCEWILL LAGANG 2023

Copyright © 2023 by Princewill Lagang

All rights reserved. No part of this publication may be reproduced, stored or transmitted in any form or by any means, electronic, mechanical, photocopying, recording, scanning, or otherwise without written permission from the publisher. It is illegal to copy this book, post it to a website, or distribute it by any other means without permission.

Princewill Lagang asserts the moral right to be identified as the author of this work.

First edition

This book was professionally typeset on Reedsy. Find out more at reedsy.com

Contents

1	Introduction	1
2	Setting the Stage	3
3	The Strategic Chessboard	6
4	Leadership Alchemy: Michael Dell's Formula for Success	9
5	Innovation at the Core: Unveiling Dell Technologies'...	12
6	Resilience and Adaptability in the Digital Age	15
7	Global Impact: Dell Technologies as a Catalyst for Change	18
8	Future Horizons: Michael Dell's Vision for Tomorrow	21
9	Legacy and Leadership Lessons	24
10	The Road Ahead: Charting Dell Technologies' Future...	27
11	Reflections on Leadership Excellence	30
12	A Conversation with Michael Dell	33
13	Epilogue - Sustaining Excellence in a Dynamic World	36
14	Summary	39

1

Introduction

In the fast-paced realm of technology and business, certain leaders emerge whose vision, resilience, and innovation shape industries and redefine possibilities. One such luminary is Michael Dell, the founder of Dell Technologies. This exploration, titled "Beyond the Boardroom: Insights into Michael Dell's Leadership and Innovation," embarks on a comprehensive journey through the life and career of Michael Dell and the transformative evolution of Dell Technologies.

In an era defined by rapid technological advancements, the narrative unfolds beyond conventional business accounts. It ventures into the intricacies of Michael Dell's leadership philosophy, strategic decisions, and the company's commitment to innovation and global impact. This exploration is not just a retrospective but an in-depth analysis of the dynamic interplay between leadership and innovation that has fueled Dell Technologies' ascent.

As we traverse the chapters, we will delve into the early influences that shaped Michael Dell, witness the birth and evolution of Dell Technologies, and scrutinize key moments that defined its trajectory. The narrative expands to encompass the company's strategic partnerships, its role in societal responsibility, and the visionary leadership that propels it into the future.

Throughout this exploration, we aim to uncover the core principles that underpin Michael Dell's leadership style, the strategies that have driven Dell Technologies to the forefront of the tech industry, and the lessons that leaders, entrepreneurs, and enthusiasts can draw from this exceptional journey. The narrative extends an invitation not just to reflect on the past but to anticipate and engage with the ever-evolving narrative of leadership and innovation that unfolds beyond the boardroom.

2

Setting the Stage

Title: Beyond the Boardroom: Insights into Michael Dell's Leadership and Innovation

The morning sun cast a warm glow over the city of Austin, Texas, as Michael Dell stepped into the bustling headquarters of Dell Technologies. The air was filled with an electric hum of anticipation, echoing the spirit of innovation that had been the driving force behind one of the world's most influential technology companies. As we embark on this journey to uncover the layers of Michael Dell's leadership and innovation, it is essential to understand the backdrop against which his remarkable story unfolds.

1.1 The Genesis of Dell Technologies

The roots of Dell Technologies trace back to the dormitory of the University of Texas at Austin in the mid-1980s. A young Michael Dell, with an insatiable curiosity for technology and an entrepreneurial spirit, started building and selling customized personal computers directly to consumers. This direct-to-consumer model marked the birth of a company that would redefine the landscape of the technology industry.

1.2 The Visionary Leader

At the heart of Dell Technologies' success is the visionary leadership of Michael Dell. We delve into his early years, exploring the experiences and influences that shaped his perspective on business and innovation. From his fascination with computers as a teenager to the strategic insights gained during the company's initial years, Michael Dell's journey unveils the makings of a leader who would challenge the status quo.

1.3 Navigating Challenges

No success story is without its share of challenges, and Michael Dell's path is no exception. This section takes a close look at the hurdles faced by Dell Technologies, from the dot-com bubble burst to the evolving dynamics of the technology market. How did Michael Dell navigate these storms, and what strategic decisions were pivotal in steering the company through turbulent times?

1.4 The Cultural Cornerstone

Beyond financial success, Dell Technologies has become synonymous with a unique corporate culture. Chapter 1 delves into the core values that have been the bedrock of the organization. From fostering a culture of innovation to emphasizing customer-centric approaches, Michael Dell's influence on the corporate ethos is explored in detail.

1.5 The Innovation Ecosystem

Innovation is woven into the fabric of Dell Technologies, and Michael Dell has been a driving force behind the company's continuous evolution. This section sheds light on the innovative initiatives spearheaded by Michael Dell, ranging from product development to strategic partnerships. How did Dell Technologies stay ahead of the curve in an ever-changing technological landscape?

1.6 Unveiling the Layers

As we conclude Chapter 1, the reader is left with a preliminary understanding of Michael Dell's leadership journey and the factors that have shaped Dell Technologies into an industry giant. The chapters that follow will unravel deeper layers, offering insights into specific strategies, challenges, and triumphs that define Michael Dell's unique approach to leadership and innovation. The story is set, the stage is illuminated, and the journey into the world of Michael Dell has just begun.

3

The Strategic Chessboard

Title: Beyond the Boardroom: Insights into Michael Dell's Leadership and Innovation

2.1 Strategic Moves: A Prelude

The chessboard of the business world is complex and ever-changing. Michael Dell's leadership is marked by strategic acumen, and this chapter delves into the early strategic moves that set the stage for Dell Technologies' ascent. From market positioning to supply chain innovations, we explore the chess pieces Michael Dell strategically placed on the board.

2.2 Direct-to-Consumer Revolution

Central to Dell Technologies' success is its disruptive direct-to-consumer model. In this section, we dissect the significance of bypassing traditional retail channels and establishing a direct link with consumers. How did this strategy not only redefine the company's business model but also influence the entire technology industry?

2.3 Adaptive Strategies for Shifting Tides

The business landscape is dynamic, and Michael Dell's leadership shines through in his ability to adapt to changing market dynamics. Whether it be shifts in consumer preferences or advancements in technology, this chapter examines the strategies employed to keep Dell Technologies at the forefront of the industry.

2.4 Mergers and Acquisitions: Crafting a Technological Tapestry

Michael Dell's approach to mergers and acquisitions has been instrumental in shaping the company's portfolio. From the acquisition of EMC to strategic partnerships, we uncover the intricacies of how Dell Technologies strategically expanded its offerings to create a comprehensive technological tapestry.

2.5 Innovation as a Strategic Imperative

Innovation is not just a buzzword at Dell Technologies; it's a strategic imperative. This section delves into the company's commitment to staying at the cutting edge of technology. From R&D investments to breakthrough product launches, Michael Dell's leadership in fostering an innovation-centric culture takes center stage.

2.6 Balancing Act: Customer-Centric Strategies

Customer satisfaction has been a cornerstone of Dell Technologies' success. This chapter explores how Michael Dell's leadership prioritizes customer-centric strategies, ensuring that the company not only meets but exceeds customer expectations. How does this focus on customer experience contribute to long-term success?

2.7 Lessons from Setbacks

No strategic journey is without setbacks. Chapter 2 examines instances where strategic moves did not go as planned and how Michael Dell navigated these challenges. What lessons were learned, and how did the setbacks contribute to the company's resilience and adaptability?

2.8 The Global Chessboard

As Dell Technologies expanded globally, the chessboard transformed into a global arena. This section explores the internationalization of the company and the strategic considerations that came with navigating diverse markets, regulatory environments, and cultural landscapes.

2.9 Looking Ahead: The Strategic Vision

The chapter concludes by peering into the future, exploring how Michael Dell's strategic vision continues to shape the company. What strategic initiatives are on the horizon, and how does the chessmaster of Dell Technologies anticipate and prepare for the next moves in the ever-evolving business landscape?

4

Leadership Alchemy: Michael Dell's Formula for Success

Title: Beyond the Boardroom: Insights into Michael Dell's Leadership and Innovation

3.1 The Art of Leadership

Great companies are often a reflection of their leaders, and Dell Technologies is no exception. This chapter delves into the artistry of Michael Dell's leadership. From his early leadership experiences to the evolution of his leadership style, we unravel the components of the alchemy that has turned Dell into an industry giant.

3.2 Leadership Foundations

Foundations matter, and Michael Dell's leadership has deep roots. This section explores the foundational principles that underpin his leadership philosophy. How have personal values, experiences, and early lessons shaped the leader who guides one of the world's most prominent technology companies?

3.3 Visionary Leadership in Action

A visionary leader sees what others cannot, and Michael Dell's journey is marked by visionary leadership in action. From foreseeing the importance of a direct-to-consumer model to anticipating technological shifts, we explore how his foresight has been a driving force in steering the company through a rapidly changing landscape.

3.4 Building and Nurturing Teams

Leadership is not a solitary pursuit, and Michael Dell understands the value of a strong team. This chapter examines how he built and nurtured teams that shared his vision. What leadership qualities does he prioritize, and how does he foster a culture that encourages innovation and collaboration?

3.5 Resilience in Leadership

The business world is rife with challenges, and resilience is a quality that defines great leaders. Michael Dell's leadership has weathered storms, and this section explores how he has demonstrated resilience in the face of adversity. What strategies does he employ to keep both himself and his team resilient?

3.6 Adaptive Leadership in a Dynamic World

Change is constant, and adaptive leadership is crucial for success. Michael Dell's leadership style is marked by adaptability and a willingness to embrace change. From technological advancements to market fluctuations, we examine how his adaptive leadership style positions Dell Technologies for continued success.

3.7 Communicating the Vision

A leader's vision is only powerful if effectively communicated. Michael Dell is known for his ability to articulate a compelling vision for the future. This section analyzes his communication style and how it resonates with both internal teams and external stakeholders. How does effective communication contribute to the alignment of the entire organization toward a common goal?

3.8 Leadership and Corporate Culture

Leadership is intertwined with corporate culture, and Michael Dell has played a pivotal role in shaping the culture at Dell Technologies. This chapter explores how his leadership philosophy aligns with the values and culture of the company. How does this alignment contribute to a cohesive and motivated workforce?

3.9 Legacy of Leadership

As we conclude Chapter 3, we reflect on the legacy of Michael Dell's leadership. What lessons can aspiring leaders draw from his journey? How has his leadership left an indelible mark on Dell Technologies, and what does it mean for the future of the company and the broader technology industry?

5

Innovation at the Core: Unveiling Dell Technologies' Technological Tapestry

Title: Beyond the Boardroom: Insights into Michael Dell's Leadership and Innovation

4.1 The Innovation Imperative

Innovation is the lifeblood of technology companies, and at the heart of Dell Technologies beats a relentless commitment to staying at the forefront of technological advancements. This chapter explores how Michael Dell's leadership has fostered a culture of innovation that permeates every facet of the organization.

4.2 R&D Investments: Fueling the Engine of Progress

Investments in research and development (R&D) are the bedrock of technological innovation. Michael Dell's approach to R&D reflects a strategic commitment to pushing the boundaries of what is possible. This section examines the significance of R&D investments in driving Dell Technologies' innovation engine.

4.3 From Hardware to Software: The Evolution of Offerings

Dell Technologies' journey goes beyond hardware. Under Michael Dell's leadership, the company has strategically expanded its offerings to include software and services. How did this evolution occur, and what strategic considerations guided the company's pivot towards a more comprehensive suite of solutions?

4.4 Transformative Technologies: AI, IoT, and Beyond

The technological landscape is marked by transformative forces such as artificial intelligence (AI) and the Internet of Things (IoT). Chapter 4 explores how Dell Technologies, under Michael Dell's guidance, has positioned itself at the intersection of these technologies. What role does the company play in shaping the future of AI, IoT, and other transformative technologies?

4.5 Sustainability and Green Innovation

In an era of heightened environmental awareness, sustainability is a critical aspect of innovation. This section delves into how Dell Technologies, under Michael Dell's leadership, has embraced green innovation. From eco-friendly product designs to sustainable business practices, we explore the company's commitment to environmental responsibility.

4.6 The Edge of Innovation: Edge Computing and Beyond

Edge computing is reshaping how we process and analyze data. This chapter examines how Dell Technologies is at the forefront of this revolution, providing insights into the strategic decisions and technological innovations that position the company as a leader in edge computing.

4.7 Strategic Partnerships: Collaborative Innovation

Innovation often thrives in collaborative ecosystems. Michael Dell has strategically forged partnerships with other industry leaders to drive innovation. This section explores the significance of these partnerships and how they contribute to Dell Technologies' ability to deliver cutting-edge solutions to its customers.

4.8 Innovation Challenges and Learnings

The path of innovation is not without challenges. Chapter 4 takes a close look at instances where innovative endeavors faced obstacles and how Michael Dell's leadership navigated these challenges. What lessons were learned, and how have setbacks contributed to the company's resilience and adaptability?

4.9 Future Horizons: The Innovation Roadmap

As we conclude this chapter, we peer into the future of innovation at Dell Technologies. What does the innovation roadmap look like under Michael Dell's leadership? How is the company poised to tackle emerging technologies, and what role will it play in shaping the technological landscape of tomorrow?

6

Resilience and Adaptability in the Digital Age

Title: Beyond the Boardroom: Insights into Michael Dell's Leadership and Innovation

5.1 Navigating the Digital Tsunami

In the era of digital transformation, businesses face a tsunami of technological disruption. This chapter explores how Michael Dell's leadership has guided Dell Technologies through the digital revolution. From cloud computing to the rise of mobile technologies, we delve into the strategic decisions that have positioned the company as a stalwart in the digital age.

5.2 Cloud Computing: A Strategic Pillar

Cloud computing has redefined the IT landscape, and Michael Dell's leadership has ensured that Dell Technologies is not just a witness but an active participant in this paradigm shift. This section examines the strategic significance of cloud computing in the company's offerings and explores how it aligns with broader industry trends.

5.3 Cybersecurity: Safeguarding the Digital Frontier

In an interconnected world, the importance of cybersecurity cannot be overstated. This chapter delves into how Michael Dell's leadership has positioned Dell Technologies as a key player in the cybersecurity space. How has the company adapted its strategies to address the evolving cybersecurity landscape, and what role does it play in safeguarding digital assets?

5.4 Digital Transformation Services

Beyond products, Dell Technologies provides a suite of services to help organizations navigate the complexities of digital transformation. This section explores the strategic initiatives and leadership decisions that have shaped the company's approach to digital transformation services. How does Dell Technologies support its clients in their journey towards a digital future?

5.5 The Remote Revolution: Dell Technologies in a Post-Pandemic World

The global shift towards remote work has accelerated, bringing new challenges and opportunities. Chapter 5 examines how Michael Dell's leadership has guided Dell Technologies through the challenges posed by the COVID-19 pandemic. How has the company adapted its strategies to support remote work and address the evolving needs of a digital workforce?

5.6 E-commerce and Changing Customer Dynamics

The rise of e-commerce has transformed how businesses interact with customers. This section explores how Dell Technologies, under Michael Dell's leadership, has adapted its strategies to align with changing customer dynamics. What role does e-commerce play in the company's business model, and how has it influenced customer engagement?

5.7 Learning from Disruption: The Dell Technologies Case

Disruptions are inevitable, but how organizations respond defines their resilience. This chapter analyzes how Dell Technologies, guided by Michael Dell's leadership, has learned from disruptive events. What lessons have been gleaned, and how has the company turned challenges into opportunities for growth and innovation?

5.8 Diversity and Inclusion in the Digital Age

The digital age brings not only technological changes but also a heightened focus on diversity and inclusion. This section explores how Michael Dell's leadership has shaped Dell Technologies' approach to diversity and inclusion. How does the company foster an inclusive workplace, and what role does diversity play in driving innovation?

5.9 The Agile Enterprise: A Vision for the Future

As we conclude this chapter, we look ahead to the future of Dell Technologies in the digital age. What is the vision for an agile enterprise under Michael Dell's leadership? How will the company continue to adapt and innovate in a rapidly evolving digital landscape?

7

Global Impact: Dell Technologies as a Catalyst for Change

Title: Beyond the Boardroom: Insights into Michael Dell's Leadership and Innovation

6.1 Beyond Business: Dell's Social Responsibility

As a global technology leader, Dell Technologies, under Michael Dell's leadership, recognizes the broader impact it can have on society. This chapter explores the company's initiatives in social responsibility, sustainability, and corporate citizenship. How does Dell Technologies leverage its influence to make a positive impact on the world beyond the boardroom?

6.2 Sustainable Business Practices

Environmental sustainability is a growing concern in the business world, and Dell Technologies is at the forefront of implementing sustainable business practices. This section examines the company's commitment to reducing its environmental footprint, from sustainable sourcing to energy efficiency initiatives. How does Michael Dell's leadership guide the company towards a more sustainable future?

6.3 Diversity, Equity, and Inclusion Initiatives

Diversity, equity, and inclusion (DEI) are crucial components of a socially responsible organization. Chapter 6 delves into how Michael Dell's leadership has influenced Dell Technologies' approach to DEI. From fostering a diverse workforce to promoting an inclusive workplace culture, we explore the initiatives that contribute to a more equitable and empowered organization.

6.4 Philanthropy and Community Engagement

A company's impact extends beyond its products and services, and Dell Technologies is actively engaged in philanthropy and community initiatives. This section explores the philanthropic endeavors supported by Michael Dell and the company. How does Dell Technologies contribute to the communities in which it operates, and what role does philanthropy play in the company's broader mission?

6.5 Bridging the Digital Divide

In an increasingly digital world, access to technology is a critical factor in determining opportunities and outcomes. This chapter examines how Michael Dell's leadership has influenced Dell Technologies' efforts to bridge the digital divide. How does the company contribute to making technology more accessible and inclusive globally?

6.6 Educational Initiatives: Empowering the Next Generation

Education is a cornerstone of social development, and Dell Technologies is actively involved in initiatives to empower the next generation. This section explores the company's contributions to education, from technology in classrooms to skills development programs. How does Michael Dell's vision extend to nurturing the skills and talents of future leaders?

6.7 Crisis Response and Humanitarian Efforts

The ability to respond effectively to crises is a measure of an organization's social responsibility. This chapter examines how Dell Technologies, guided by Michael Dell's leadership, has played a role in crisis response and humanitarian efforts. How does the company contribute to global well-being during times of crisis?

6.8 Corporate Governance and Ethical Leadership

Beyond philanthropy, corporate governance and ethical leadership are fundamental aspects of social responsibility. This section explores how Michael Dell's leadership has shaped the company's commitment to ethical business practices and strong corporate governance. What measures are in place to ensure accountability and transparency in Dell Technologies' operations?

6.9 Shaping a Better Future

As we conclude this chapter, we reflect on Dell Technologies' role as a catalyst for positive change under Michael Dell's leadership. How does the company contribute to shaping a better future for society, and what lessons can be drawn from its socially responsible initiatives?

8

Future Horizons: Michael Dell's Vision for Tomorrow

Title: Beyond the Boardroom: Insights into Michael Dell's Leadership and Innovation

7.1 Anticipating the Future: A Visionary's Lens

The ability to foresee and adapt to the future is a hallmark of great leadership. This chapter delves into Michael Dell's visionary outlook and how his leadership anticipates the challenges and opportunities that lie ahead. What key trends and technologies does he foresee shaping the future, and how is Dell Technologies positioned to navigate this landscape?

7.2 Evolving Business Models: The Shape of Tomorrow

The business landscape is undergoing rapid transformation, and Dell Technologies is at the forefront of adapting its business models to meet the demands of tomorrow. This section explores the evolution of business models under Michael Dell's leadership. How is the company positioned to thrive in an era of continuous change and disruption?

7.3 Emerging Technologies: A Glimpse into the Future

The technological landscape is dynamic, with emerging technologies shaping industries and societies. Chapter 7 delves into how Michael Dell's leadership positions Dell Technologies at the forefront of emerging technologies. From quantum computing to 6G connectivity, we explore the company's strategies for staying ahead in a rapidly evolving tech environment.

7.4 The Impact of Artificial Intelligence

Artificial intelligence (AI) is a transformative force with far-reaching implications. This section examines Michael Dell's perspective on the role of AI in shaping the future and how Dell Technologies is harnessing AI to drive innovation. What are the ethical considerations, and how is the company contributing to responsible AI development?

7.5 Transformative Industries: Dell Technologies as a Catalyst

Industries across the globe are undergoing digital transformation, and Dell Technologies plays a pivotal role as a catalyst for this change. This chapter explores how the company, under Michael Dell's leadership, contributes to the transformation of industries such as healthcare, finance, and manufacturing. How does Dell Technologies empower businesses to embrace digital innovation?

7.6 Cybersecurity in the Future Landscape

As technology advances, so do the threats in the digital landscape. This section examines Michael Dell's vision for the future of cybersecurity and how Dell Technologies is innovating to stay ahead of cyber threats. How is the company working to create a secure digital environment for businesses and individuals?

7.7 The Role of Sustainability in Tomorrow's Business

Sustainability is no longer just a choice but a necessity for businesses looking to thrive in the future. Chapter 7 explores Michael Dell's vision for sustainability and how Dell Technologies is integrating sustainable practices into its business strategies. What is the company's role in promoting a sustainable and responsible approach to business?

7.8 Shaping the Future Workforce

The workforce of the future will require new skills and perspectives. This section examines Michael Dell's perspective on the future of work and how Dell Technologies is contributing to shaping a future-ready workforce. What initiatives are in place to foster continuous learning and skill development?

7.9 The Next Chapter: Dell Technologies in the Decades to Come

As we conclude this chapter, we gaze into the crystal ball of Dell Technologies' future. What is Michael Dell's vision for the company in the decades to come? How will Dell Technologies continue to lead, innovate, and contribute to the ever-evolving world of technology and business?

9

Legacy and Leadership Lessons

Title: Beyond the Boardroom: Insights into Michael Dell's Leadership and Innovation

8.1 The Legacy of Michael Dell

A leader's impact extends beyond their tenure, and Michael Dell's legacy is woven into the fabric of Dell Technologies and the broader technology industry. This chapter reflects on the enduring legacy of Michael Dell and how his leadership has left an indelible mark on the company, its employees, and the world of business.

8.2 Lessons from Leadership

Leadership is a continuous journey of growth and learning. This section distills key leadership lessons from Michael Dell's journey. What principles, values, and practices have contributed to his success as a leader? How can aspiring leaders draw inspiration from his experiences to navigate their own leadership paths?

8.3 The Evolution of Leadership in the Digital Age

The digital age has reshaped the expectations of leaders. This chapter examines how Michael Dell's leadership style has evolved in response to the challenges and opportunities presented by the digital landscape. What qualities are essential for leaders navigating the complexities of the digital age?

8.4 Leadership in Times of Crisis

Crisis reveals the true mettle of leaders. This section explores how Michael Dell's leadership has manifested during times of crisis, from economic downturns to global pandemics. What strategies has he employed to lead Dell Technologies through turbulent times, and what lessons can be drawn for leaders facing adversity?

8.5 Balancing Innovation and Tradition

Innovation is a driving force, but tradition and core values anchor an organization. Chapter 8 delves into how Michael Dell has navigated the delicate balance between fostering innovation and preserving the core values that define Dell Technologies. How has this balance contributed to the company's sustained success?

8.6 Leadership and Corporate Culture: A Symbiotic Relationship

Leadership and corporate culture are intertwined, shaping the character of an organization. This section examines how Michael Dell's leadership philosophy aligns with and influences the corporate culture at Dell Technologies. How does a positive culture reinforce effective leadership, and vice versa?

8.7 The Human Side of Leadership

Leadership is fundamentally about people. This chapter explores the human side of Michael Dell's leadership—his approach to team building, mentorship, and fostering a collaborative work environment. How has his focus on the human aspect contributed to a motivated and engaged workforce?

8.8 Challenges as Catalysts for Growth

Challenges are inevitable, but how leaders respond to them determines their trajectory. This section examines how Michael Dell has turned challenges into opportunities for growth. What resilience strategies has he employed, and how have setbacks ultimately propelled Dell Technologies forward?

8.9 The Enduring Spirit of Innovation

As we conclude this chapter, we reflect on the enduring spirit of innovation that permeates Michael Dell's leadership journey. How has his commitment to innovation shaped Dell Technologies, and what does it signify for the company's future? What enduring principles will continue to guide the organization as it evolves in the years to come?

10

The Road Ahead: Charting Dell Technologies' Future Trajectory

Title: Beyond the Boardroom: Insights into Michael Dell's Leadership and Innovation

9.1 Forward into the Future

As Michael Dell's leadership journey continues to unfold, this chapter peers into the road ahead for Dell Technologies. What strategic initiatives are on the horizon, and how will the company navigate the ever-evolving landscape of technology, business, and global challenges? This section sets the stage for the future trajectory of Dell Technologies.

9.2 Strategic Growth and Expansion

Strategic growth is essential for any organization seeking to thrive in the future. This section explores Michael Dell's vision for the strategic growth and expansion of Dell Technologies. What markets, industries, and technologies are the focus of the company's growth strategy, and how does it plan to stay ahead of the curve?

9.3 Digital Transformation at Scale

Digital transformation is not a destination but an ongoing journey. Chapter 9 delves into how Dell Technologies, under Michael Dell's leadership, envisions digital transformation at scale. How will the company continue to support organizations in their digital journeys, and what role will emerging technologies play in this transformative landscape?

9.4 Continued Commitment to Innovation

Innovation remains a cornerstone of Dell Technologies' success. This section examines how the company plans to sustain its commitment to innovation. What investments in research and development are on the horizon, and how will Dell Technologies harness emerging technologies to drive continuous innovation?

9.5 Global Impact and Social Responsibility

As a global leader, Dell Technologies has the power to make a positive impact on society. This chapter explores how Michael Dell envisions the company's role in global impact and social responsibility. What initiatives will continue to drive sustainability, diversity, and community engagement in the years to come?

9.6 Shaping the Future Workforce

The workforce is evolving, and Dell Technologies recognizes the importance of shaping a future-ready workforce. This section delves into the company's strategies for talent development, upskilling, and fostering a workplace culture that adapts to the changing dynamics of the modern workforce.

9.7 Partnerships and Collaborations

Collaborations with industry partners are instrumental in navigating the complex technology landscape. Chapter 9 explores Michael Dell's vision for partnerships and collaborations. How will Dell Technologies strengthen existing partnerships and forge new alliances to drive mutual innovation and growth?

9.8 Customer-Centric Strategies

Customer satisfaction remains a top priority for Dell Technologies. This section examines how the company plans to enhance customer-centric strategies. What innovations in customer experience are on the horizon, and how will Dell Technologies continue to meet the evolving needs of its diverse customer base?

9.9 Leadership Continuity and Succession Planning

Leadership continuity is crucial for the sustained success of any organization. As Michael Dell's leadership journey continues, this chapter explores the company's approach to leadership continuity and succession planning. How is Dell Technologies preparing for a seamless transition to the next generation of leaders?

9.10 The Ever-Adapting Chessboard

As we conclude this chapter, we reflect on the metaphorical chessboard of the business world—an ever-adapting landscape where strategic moves determine success. What does the future hold for Dell Technologies on this dynamic board, and how will Michael Dell's leadership continue to guide the company through the twists and turns of the road ahead?

11

Reflections on Leadership Excellence

Title: Beyond the Boardroom: Insights into Michael Dell's Leadership and Innovation

10.1 Leadership Excellence: A Retrospective

As we reach the final chapter, we reflect on the overarching theme of leadership excellence that defines Michael Dell's journey. This section revisits key moments, decisions, and attributes that have shaped his leadership legacy. What elements of leadership excellence stand out, and how have they contributed to the success of Dell Technologies?

10.2 Leadership in the Technology Landscape

The technology landscape is unforgiving, marked by rapid change and fierce competition. This chapter examines Michael Dell's unique approach to leadership within this dynamic industry. How has he navigated the challenges and harnessed the opportunities presented by the ever-evolving world of technology?

10.3 The Human Element: Leadership in a People-Centric World

Leadership is fundamentally about people, and Michael Dell's journey has been marked by a people-centric approach. This section explores how he has fostered a culture that values individuals, nurtures talent, and prioritizes the well-being of the workforce. How has this focus on the human element contributed to Dell Technologies' success?

10.4 Innovation as a Guiding Principle

Innovation is not just a strategic imperative at Dell Technologies; it is a guiding principle. This chapter reflects on how Michael Dell's commitment to innovation has shaped the company's culture, products, and industry influence. How has innovation been woven into the very fabric of Dell Technologies under his leadership?

10.5 Navigating Change: Lessons in Adaptability

Change is constant, and adaptability is a hallmark of effective leadership. This section revisits instances where Michael Dell's leadership demonstrated agility and adaptability in the face of industry shifts, economic changes, and global challenges. What lessons can be drawn from his ability to navigate change with resilience?

10.6 Building a Lasting Legacy

Leadership excellence is measured not just by current success but by the lasting legacy a leader leaves behind. Chapter 10 examines how Michael Dell has positioned Dell Technologies for long-term success and influence. What elements of his leadership will continue to shape the company's trajectory well into the future?

10.7 The Global Impact of Dell Technologies

Dell Technologies is a global player, influencing industries, communities, and the technology sector at large. This section explores the global impact of the company under Michael Dell's leadership. How has Dell Technologies contributed to global innovation, sustainability, and societal well-being?

10.8 Leadership and Corporate Responsibility

Corporate responsibility goes hand in hand with leadership excellence. This chapter reflects on how Michael Dell has infused principles of responsibility, ethics, and social impact into the fabric of Dell Technologies. How has the company's leadership championed responsible business practices and corporate citizenship?

10.9 Inspiring the Next Generation of Leaders

Leadership excellence extends beyond the present, inspiring future generations of leaders. This section examines Michael Dell's role in shaping the leadership landscape for the next generation. How has his journey served as a source of inspiration and guidance for emerging leaders in the technology and business sectors?

10.10 Closing Thoughts: A Legacy of Leadership and Innovation

As we conclude this exploration into Michael Dell's leadership and innovation, we reflect on the enduring legacy he has created at Dell Technologies. This final section offers closing thoughts on the impact of his leadership, the lessons learned, and the ongoing journey of Dell Technologies in a world where the only constant is change.

12

A Conversation with Michael Dell

Title: Beyond the Boardroom: Insights into Michael Dell's Leadership and Innovation

11.1 Setting the Stage

In this unique chapter, we have the privilege of engaging in a conversation with Michael Dell himself. As the visionary leader behind Dell Technologies, he shares personal insights, reflections, and perspectives on various aspects of his leadership journey and the future of the company.

11.2 Early Influences and Formative Experiences

Our conversation begins by delving into the early influences and formative experiences that shaped Michael Dell's perspective on leadership and innovation. What were the pivotal moments in his early life that set the stage for his entrepreneurial journey and the founding of Dell Technologies?

11.3 Navigating Challenges: A Leader's Perspective

Challenges are inevitable in any leadership journey. Michael Dell shares his insights on navigating challenges, overcoming setbacks, and turning adversity into opportunities. How does he approach challenges, and what strategies has he employed to lead Dell Technologies through periods of change and uncertainty?

11.4 The Evolution of Dell Technologies

As we explore the evolution of Dell Technologies, Michael Dell provides his perspective on the company's growth, strategic decisions, and the factors that have contributed to its success. How has the company transformed over the years, and what role has innovation played in its journey?

11.5 Leadership Philosophy and Values

Leadership is deeply rooted in personal philosophy and values. Michael Dell discusses his leadership philosophy, the core values that guide his decision-making, and the principles that have shaped the culture at Dell Technologies. How do these values align with the company's vision and mission?

11.6 Vision for the Future

Looking forward, Michael Dell shares his vision for the future of Dell Technologies. What emerging technologies, industry trends, and global challenges does he foresee shaping the company's trajectory? How is Dell Technologies positioned to continue leading in an ever-evolving technology landscape?

11.7 The Human Element in Leadership

A central theme throughout our conversation is the importance of the human element in leadership. Michael Dell elaborates on the significance of building strong teams, fostering a positive corporate culture, and prioritizing the well-being of employees. How does he balance the human element with the demands of the tech industry?

11.8 Global Impact and Social Responsibility

Dell Technologies has a global footprint, and Michael Dell discusses the company's commitment to making a positive impact on society. From environmental sustainability to social responsibility initiatives, how does he envision Dell Technologies contributing to a better world?

11.9 Leadership Legacy and Advice for Aspiring Leaders

Reflecting on his leadership journey, Michael Dell shares thoughts on the legacy he hopes to leave behind and imparts advice for aspiring leaders. What lessons has he learned throughout his career, and what wisdom does he offer to those who aim to make a mark in the world of business and technology?

11.10 Closing Remarks

As we conclude this insightful conversation, Michael Dell shares final thoughts, expressing gratitude for the journey, highlighting key takeaways, and leaving readers with inspiration for their own leadership endeavors. This chapter serves as a unique opportunity to gain direct insights from the leader himself, bringing a personal touch to the exploration of leadership and innovation at Dell Technologies.

13

Epilogue - Sustaining Excellence in a Dynamic World

Title: Beyond the Boardroom: Insights into Michael Dell's Leadership and Innovation

12.1 Reflecting on the Journey

In this final chapter, we reflect on the comprehensive exploration of Michael Dell's leadership and Dell Technologies' journey. From the inception of the company to its current position as a global technology giant, we revisit key insights, lessons, and milestones that define the narrative of innovation and leadership excellence.

12.2 The Ever-Evolving Landscape

The business and technology landscape is in a constant state of evolution. This section examines the ongoing changes in the industry and the broader global context. How has Dell Technologies adapted to the ever-evolving landscape, and what strategies are in place to ensure continued relevance and

EPILOGUE - SUSTAINING EXCELLENCE IN A DYNAMIC WORLD

success?

12.3 Nurturing a Culture of Innovation

One of the central themes throughout this narrative has been the emphasis on innovation. We explore how Michael Dell's leadership has fostered a culture of innovation within Dell Technologies. What mechanisms are in place to encourage creativity, exploration, and the continual pursuit of groundbreaking ideas?

12.4 Resilience and Adaptability as Pillars of Strength

Resilience and adaptability have been recurring themes in the story of Dell Technologies. This section delves into how these qualities have become integral to the company's DNA. How does Dell Technologies remain resilient in the face of challenges, and how does it proactively adapt to stay ahead of the curve?

12.5 Lessons for Leaders and Entrepreneurs

As we conclude the exploration into Michael Dell's leadership journey, this section distills key lessons for current and aspiring leaders and entrepreneurs. What principles, strategies, and values can they draw inspiration from to navigate their own paths to success in a rapidly changing business landscape?

12.6 Future Horizons: Dell Technologies Beyond Today

Looking to the future, we contemplate the potential trajectories for Dell Technologies. What strategic initiatives, technological innovations, and leadership principles will define the company's future trajectory? How will Dell Technologies continue to shape the industry and contribute to global progress?

12.7 The Enduring Legacy of Leadership Excellence

Legacy endures beyond the present, and this section reflects on the enduring legacy of Michael Dell's leadership and its impact on Dell Technologies. How will his contributions continue to shape the company's ethos and influence the broader landscape of business, technology, and corporate responsibility?

12.8 A Call to Action: Inspiring Leadership and Innovation

In the closing remarks, we issue a call to action inspired by the insights gained from Michael Dell's journey. How can leaders, organizations, and innovators apply these lessons to inspire positive change, foster innovation, and contribute to the betterment of the global community?

12.9 Acknowledgments and Gratitude

This chapter concludes with expressions of gratitude to the individuals, collaborators, and contributors who have played a role in bringing this exploration to life. The collective effort reflects the spirit of collaboration and learning that underlies the narrative of leadership and innovation at Dell Technologies.

12.10 Beyond the Boardroom: A Continuing Narrative

As we bid farewell to this exploration, we acknowledge that the narrative of leadership and innovation at Dell Technologies is an ongoing journey. This section encourages readers to stay engaged with the evolving story of Dell Technologies, Michael Dell's leadership, and the broader dynamics of the business and technology landscape.

In closing, "Beyond the Boardroom" stands not just as a retrospective but as an invitation to continue exploring the limitless horizons of leadership and innovation in the dynamic world that lies ahead.

14

Summary

"Beyond the Boardroom: Insights into Michael Dell's Leadership and Innovation" is a comprehensive exploration spanning twelve chapters that provides a deep dive into the life, leadership, and innovative journey of Michael Dell, the founder of Dell Technologies. The narrative unfolds through various dimensions, including leadership philosophy, strategic decisions, innovation, global impact, and social responsibility. Each chapter explores specific facets such as Michael Dell's early influences, the evolution of Dell Technologies, the company's commitment to sustainability, and its role in shaping the future of technology.

The book begins with an introduction that sets the stage for an in-depth examination of Michael Dell's leadership style and the factors that have propelled Dell Technologies to its prominent position in the technology industry. Subsequent chapters delve into Michael Dell's early years, the formation of Dell Technologies, and his visionary approach to leadership and innovation.

The exploration extends into the realms of corporate culture, resilience, and adaptability, showcasing how these elements have been instrumental in steering Dell Technologies through challenges and technological transformations. The book also scrutinizes Dell Technologies' commitment to innovation, strategic partnerships, and the continuous evolution of its product and service offerings.

Chapters dedicated to the company's global impact, social responsibility, and initiatives in diversity and inclusion underscore the significance of Dell Technologies beyond business. The narrative concludes with a forward-looking perspective on the future of Dell Technologies under Michael Dell's leadership, emphasizing the importance of sustainability, workforce development, and the ever-changing landscape of technology.

The book culminates in a unique chapter featuring a conversation with Michael Dell, offering readers direct insights into his thoughts on leadership, innovation, and the future trajectory of Dell Technologies. The epilogue reflects on the journey, distills key lessons, and emphasizes the enduring legacy of leadership excellence.

"Beyond the Boardroom" is not only a retrospective but also an invitation to readers to stay engaged with the evolving narrative of Dell Technologies, leadership, and innovation in the dynamic world that lies ahead.

www.ingramcontent.com/pod-product-compliance
Lightning Source LLC
LaVergne TN
LVHW012131070526
838202LV00056B/5956